KAAKULUK

INSIDE THIS ISSUE:

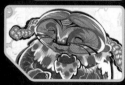
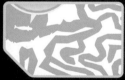

Cover Illustration: Anthony Brennan

In this issue of Kaakuluk, we feature a myth from the Qikiqtani region. It is called **How Caribou and Walrus came to be**.

THE BELUGA WHALE?

class: Mammal
species: Delphinapterus leucas
length: up to 5 metres
weight: 900 kg - 1 360 kg

" I'VE SEEN WHALES ON TV AND I'VE SEEN WHALES IN CAPE DORSET. AND I LIKE WHALES. " Naiumie Curley, Iqaluit

" I ATE A WHALE, FROZEN STYLE. WHEN I WENT TO GO ON A VACATION TO GRISE FIORD, I SAW LOTS OF CAUGHT WHALES. THERE WERE LITTLE YELLOWISH-ORANGISH BUGS (ON THE WHALES). " Natasha Madline Akeeagok, Iqaluit

" WHALES EAT FISH. PEOPLE HUNT THE WHALES AND EAT THEM. I ATE SOME BEFORE." Jaja Esnaja, Iqaluit

"MOST OF THE PEOPLE LIKE TO EAT WHALES BECAUSE THEY ARE VERY GOOD!" Teresa Qiatsuq, Iqaluit

WORDS OF WISDOM

from Jonny Karetak

Johnny Karetak is an elder from Arviat. Adriana Kusugak interviewed him about beluga whales. The following is an excerpt from their interview.

How long have you been hunting whales?

When I was about five or six years old I followed others who were hunting whales. I watched, observed, and helped the others who were hunting the whales.

What are the differences between then and now?

It has not changed much but it seems as though they are more careless now when hunting whales. People take off too much "uqsuq"- whale fat. Uqsuq makes the muktaaq taste much better. When there isn't enough uqsuq the maktaaq doesn't taste as good and goes bad. Uqsuq preserves the taste. Hunters nowadays say it is just extra weight, but it makes and preserves that great taste of muktaaq.

They say beluga whales sing. Did you ever hear them and what does it sound like?

Yes, I have heard them. You can hear them when whales are not aware of hunters around them in shallow areas. When we heard them we did not chase them right away. It was when the tide was going up. Sometimes they seem to come up out of the water and whistle. They seem to play too with their blowhole.

Are belugas hard to hunt?

It can be but you have to try to get them to shallow areas. You have to be patient to see where they are going. You have to steer them to shallow areas. You steer them and you can follow the whales to ensure you don't hit any rocks while travelling in shallow areas.

What are some techniques you use to make sure the hunt is successful?

You have to try and get them to shallow waters. Here in the Kivalliq, because it is shallow here, you have to be quiet. Whales seem to have very sensitive hearing and can hear when boats and hunters are near if they make too much noise. You just know sometimes when you are going to catch something. You have to stay focused on the whale and go for the one you want. The younger ones taste the best. They are not all white but are not totally grey either.

When do whales have the most fat?

In the winter the whales have the most fat. You can tell when whales are very fat because they don't sink.

When is the best season to hunt whales?

From the middle to the end of August to the beginning of September is when whales taste best.

Kevin Schafer

BELUGA Q&A

Q: WHAT DO THEY LOOK LIKE?

The beluga is a small, toothed whale that is completely white as an adult. Its body is stout and it has a blunt, rounded head. The beluga does not have a dorsal fin (top fin). It has thick layers of blubber on its body and one blowhole near the top of its head. Unlike most whales, the beluga's neck bones are not stuck together. This gives the beluga a flexible, well defined neck.

Belugas can reach 5 metres in length, which is small for whales. The males can weigh up to 1360 kgs. Female belugas are a little smaller, weighing up to 900 kgs.

Q: DO THEY HAVE TEETH?

Yes, beluga whales have 34 teeth in their mouths. These teeth are designed for grabbing and tearing prey, not chewing. Belugas swallow their prey whole.

Q: ARE THEY FRIENDLY WITH EACH OTHER?

Yes, beluga whales are very social animals. They gather in groups of about ten whales. A group of beluga whales is called a pod. These pods can be made up of males and females or mothers and calves. A pod of beluga whales will hunt and migrate together. In fact, sometimes when beluga whales are migrating, different pods group together, forming groups of up to 10,000 whales.

Q: ARE THEY FAST SWIMMERS?

No, belugas are relatively slow swimmers when compared to other whales. They swim about 3 to 9 kilometres per hour. When they need to, they can speed up to 22 kilometres per hour, but only for a short time.

Q: DO THEY MAKE SOUNDS?

Yes! Belugas are amongst the loudest animals in the sea. They produce many different sounds, such as clicks, squeals, and whistles. You can even hear these sounds above the water. Because of the beluga's ability to make sounds, they are sometimes called "sea canaries." Belugas use sound to find prey, to find breathing holes in the ice and to navigate in deep, dark water. Belugas make clicking sounds and listen for these sounds to bounce off of objects. They can estimate the distance of an object by the length of time it takes for their clicks to bounce back to them. Using sound like this is called echolocation.

Q: ARE THEY GOOD DIVERS?

Yes, beluga whales can dive to a depth of about 650 metres, but more commonly they dive about 20 metres below the surface to find food. They can stay under water for about 20 minutes. While underwater, a beluga can travel about 2.5 kilometres before coming back up for air.

Q: HOW LONG DO THEY LIVE?

Beluga whales usually live between 25 and 30 years.

Besides humans, orcas (killer whales) and polar bear prey on belugas, especially the baby belugas.

Belugas are opportunistic feeders. This means that they are not picky and eat whatever comes along. Usually, a beluga's diet consists of a variety of fish, squid, crustaceans, octopi and marine worms. Sometimes, belugas hunt schools of fish in small groups. Adult belugas eat about 25 kgs of food a day. That's a lot of seafood!

Baby belugas, called calves, are born after being in their mothers' womb for about 15 months. They are born in shallow, warm water and instinctively swim to the surface to breath. The mother helps her baby to the surface with her flippers.

Beluga calves are between 1.2 and 1.5 metres in length and can weigh over 60 kgs. Usually, only one beluga calf is born per birth, but sometimes twins are born.

Photographs: Kevin Schafer

The Beluga Whale:
Traditional Uses

Beluga whales are important to our way of life. We use beluga in a variety of ways. Here are some of the ways each of the different parts of the beluga can be used.

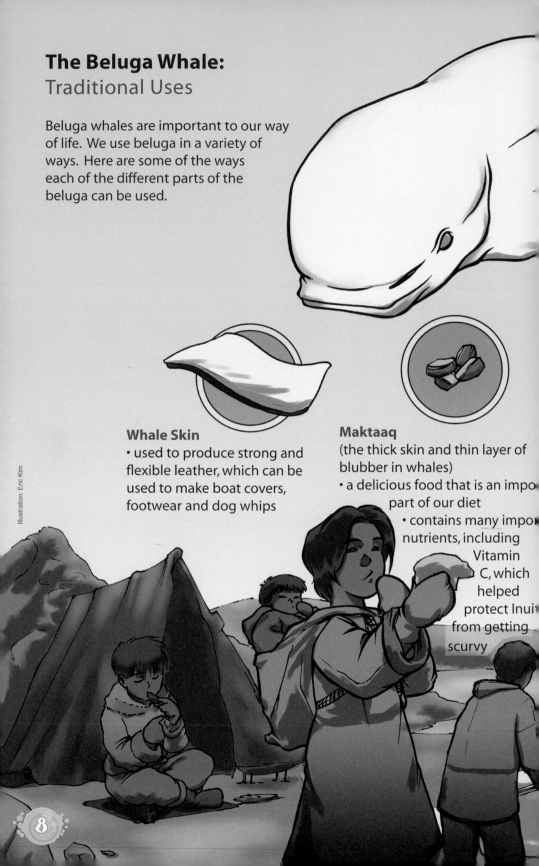

Whale Skin
• used to produce strong and flexible leather, which can be used to make boat covers, footwear and dog whips

Maktaaq
(the thick skin and thin layer of blubber in whales)
• a delicious food that is an impo part of our diet
• contains many impo nutrients, including Vitamin C, which helped protect Inui from getting scurvy

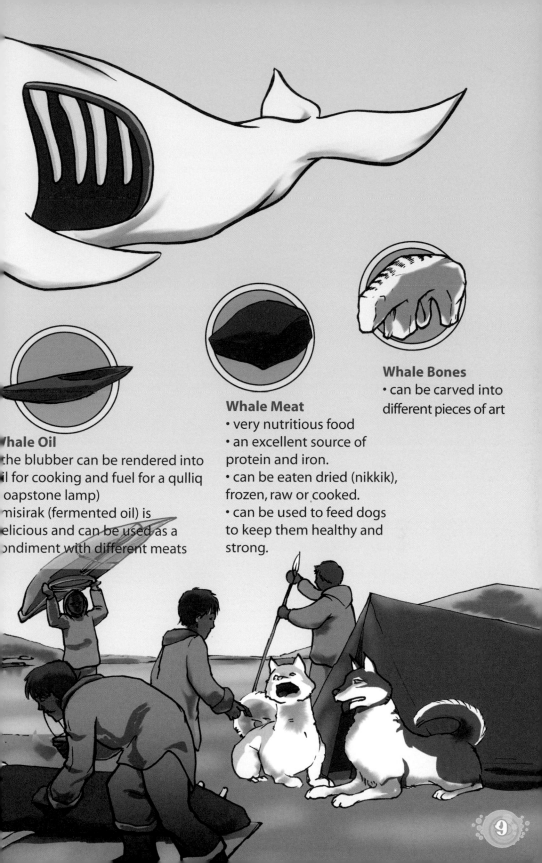

Whale Bones
• can be carved into different pieces of art

Whale Meat
• very nutritious food
• an excellent source of protein and iron.
• can be eaten dried (nikkik), frozen, raw or cooked.
• can be used to feed dogs to keep them healthy and strong.

Whale Oil
the blubber can be rendered into oil for cooking and fuel for a qulliq (soapstone lamp)
misirak (fermented oil) is delicious and can be used as a condiment with different meats

Help this beluga whale navigate the icy water to find the other whales of its pod.

HELP ME FIND MY POD!

How the Caribou and Walrus Came To Be

Illustrations: Anthony Brennan

This story happened somewhere in the Arctic, a very long time ago.

Once, an old woman was sitting in her home and thought to herself: "We need more animals to hunt. We need more animals to feed our families and hides to keep us warm during the winter."

So, she said, "I will transform my old seal-skin jacket into a walrus!"
And she did just that - she made a walrus. She looked at it and
thought that it didn't look quite right. So, she put antlers on its
head and she put it into the water. And it looked very well.

She then said to herself, "I will transform my trousers into a caribou!" And she did just that - she made a caribou. Once again, she looked at it and thought that it didn't look quite right. So, she put tusks in its mouth and she set it free. And it looked very well.

One day the caribou saw a hunter coming towards it. The caribou wasn't afraid of this man, so it ran up to him and injured the hunter with its tusks. The injured hunter ran all the way home and told the community what had happened.

When the hunter told the old lady of his scary adventure, she became very angry.

She called the caribou and the walrus, and they came to her. She took the antlers from the walrus and put them on the caribou's head. She took the tusks from the caribou and gave them to the walrus. And they looked very well.

She said to the caribou, "You shall never come near the walrus. You will stay far away inland and whenever you will smell the scent of a hunter you will be afraid!"

And this is how the walrus and the caribou came to inhabit our land.

Spot the Difference

There are six differences between these images. Can you spot them?

www.INUITMYTHS.com

The Qikiqtani Inuit Association (QIA) work hard to promote and protect Inuit culture QIA has developed Inuitmyths.com to provide a resource for Nunavummiut and people from around the world who wan to learn more about the Inuit storytelling tradition.

Our project partners are:
Canadian Heritage • Nunavut Bilingual Education Society
Nunavut Teacher Education Program • Nunavut Arctic College
Department of Culture, Language, Elders and Youth
Department of Education • Canadian Broadcasting Corporation

KAAKULUK

Presented by
Qikiqtani Inuit Association
Nunavut Bilingual Education Society

Publisher: Neil Christopher
Editors: Louise Flaherty (Inuktitut)
        Stephanie McDonald (English)
Art Director: Danny Christopher
Translator: Louise Flaherty
Contributing Educator: Neevee Hanson
Thanks: To the students of Joamie School in Iqaluit who shared their thoughts and experiences about beluga whales with Kaakuluk magazine.

Kaakuluk is available to schools throughout the Qikiqtani region of Nunavut thanks to the financial support of Canadian Heritage.

All materials © 2008 Inhabit Media Inc.

For more information please contact:

Becky Kilabuk (QIA Youth Coordinator) youth@qia.ca
or
Neil Christopher (NBES)
info@nbes.ca

Inhabit Media Inc.
P.O.Box 11125, Iqaluit, NU, X0A 1H0

Answers from pages 17

 Canadian   Patrimoine
Heritage   canadien

www.INUITMYTHS.com

ᕴᑭᕞᑕᓂ ᐃᓄᐃᑦ ᑲᑐᔾᖄᑲᑎᒌᖁᑦ (QIA
ᐊᑯᓲᖅᑐᑎ ᐱᓕᓕᐊᖅᖅᐸᒻᒪᑕ ᐃᓄᐃᑦ
ᐃᓕᖅᑯᓯᖑᓕᓂᖅ ᕼᖅᑅᖅᕿᑕᑎᑕᓂᐊᖅᑐ
ᕼᐳᒡᑎᓐᑎᓯᑦᐊᖅᑐᑎᓐᒡ. QIA
ᕼᕿᑥᔪᒡᒻᒍᒻᒪᑕ Inuitmyths.com
ᐊᑐᓐᕼᐸᖅᖃᓂᕼᑎᑎᑎᒡᑐᑎ ᓄᐊᕿᒻᒪ
ᓄᐊᕐᖁᐊᒻᑌᓂᒡᑦ ᐃᑕᑦᖃᓂᒻᐅᔪᖅ
ᐃᓄᐃᑦ ᐅᓂᒃᑲᖅᑐᐊᕐᑎᓂᖅ.

ᐱᓕᓕᖅᑲᑎᑉᕈᕞᑕᖅᒡ:
ᖄᑕᒻᒪ ᐱᖅᑯᓴᓯᑎᕤᖅᑯᑦ* ᓄᐊᕿᒻᒪ ᒪᔾᖔᓂᖅ ᐅᖅᑲᐅᓯᓐᓇᓂᖅ
ᐃᑳᓯᓇᐊᖅᑎᑎᓂᔾᒡᑌ ᑲᑐᔾᖄᑲᑎᖅᑦ
ᓄᐊᕿᒻᒪ ᐃᑲᕼᐃᔪᕼᖅᑕᑦ ᐃᑳᓯᓇᐊᕿᖃᓕᑦ*ᓄᐊᕿᑦ ᕼᓚᑐᑦᖅᕼᖅᖅᑎᕼ
ᐃᓯᖅᑯᓯᓯᓂᐊᖅᑦ
ᐃᑳᓯᓇᐊᕼᓂᑎᓂᔾᖅᑦᒡᑦ-ᖄᑕᒻᒪ ᑐᑭᓯᕼᓯᓂᐊᖅᑦ

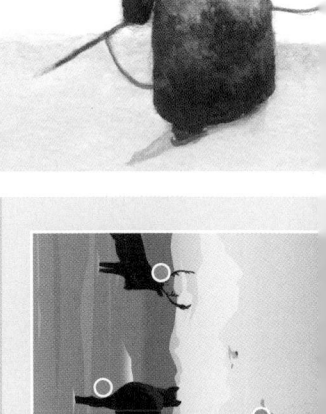

ᕼᕿᑭᑕᐅᕼᖅ ᐅᑯᓄᒡᑦ
ᓄᐊᕿᒻᒪ ᒪᔾᖔᓂᖅ ᐅᖅᑲᐅᓯᓐᓇᓂᖅ
ᐃᑳᓯᓇᐊᖅᑎᑎᓂᔾᒡᑌ ᑲᑐᔾᖄᑲᑎᖏᑦ

ᕼᕿᑥᕞᖅ: ᓂᑦ ᑎᓄᕐᑕᐅᑦ
ᐊᕼᖅᑭᕈᐊᓯᖅ: ᑐᐃᓯ ᕼᑦᒪᐅᕼᑎ
(ᐃᓄ�|ᑎᑐᑦ)
ᕼᑎᑎᖁᓂ ᒪᖃᐃᓄᑐ (ᖅᖃᑐᐅᓇᑎᑎᑦ)
ᑕᑎᒌᓯᑐᑦᒪᓂᐸ ᑐᖁᓚᐊᕼᑎᑎᑎᖅᕞ: ᑦᓂ
ᑎᓄᕐᑕᐅᑦ
ᐃᓄᑲᑎᓯᑐᕼᖅᑎᑎᑎᑲᑕ: ᑐᐃᓯ ᕼᑦᒪᐅᕼᑎ
ᐃᑲᕼᕼᒻᒡᕕᖅ ᐃᑳᓯᓇᐊᖅᑎᑎᑎᕞ: ᑦᓇ
ᕼᐊᕞᕼ

ᕼᑦᒪᓐᑌᖅᕼᑕᖅ: ᕴᒻ ᐃᑳᓯᓇᐊᖅᕞᒻᒻ
ᐃᑳᓯᓇᐊᖅᕼᖅᑦ ᑎᖅᑐᓇᕼᖅ
ᐃᓯᒪᕤᕼᔾᓂᖅᖅᓂᒡᑦ ᐊᐊᑦᑐᐊᖅᒡ
ᐊᑎᒻᕼᑦᔾᒡᕼᓂᕼᖅᒡᔾ ᕼᖅᐅᕞᒻᖅᑕᑦ

ᒻᒥᕼᓂᒡᑦ ᑲᑯᓂᒡ ᐅᕼᑲᑦᒻᒻᑌᔾᒡ.

ᕼᑲᑎᕼᕼ ᐊᑐᐃᒪᕕᐅᕼᖅ
ᐃᑳᓯᓇᐊᕼᑲᖅᓚᑎᑎᑦ ᕴᑭᕞᑕᓂ
ᓄᐊᕼᐅᑑᓂᑲ ᕼᑕᑦᖃᑲᖅᖃᕼᐸᑦ
ᖄᑕᒻᒪ ᐱᖅᑯᓴᓯᑎᕤᒻᒡᑦ.

ᐊᑎᖅᑕᐅᑐᑦ c. 2008 Inhabit
Media Inc.

ᑐᑭᕤᑲᐅᑲᖅᓂᕼᔾᕼᒻ
ᕼᑥᕼᐊᖅᖃᑐᑎᕤᑲ:
ᐃᕞᐸ ᕼᕼᑕᕼᖁᓐᔾᒡᑌ (QIA
ᒪᖅᑯᑐᑎᓯ) youth@qia.ca
ᐅᕼᖃᔾᓂᓂᒡ
ᓂᑦ ᑎᓄᕐᑕᐅᑦ (NBES)
infor@nbes.ca

Inhabit media Inc.
P.O. Box 11125, Iqaluit, NU,
X0A 1H0

ᑭᓄᒻᑐᑎᑦ ᒪᕼᐱᒡᕼᖅ 17ᒡᑦ (answers

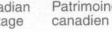 Canadian Heritage Patrimoine canadien

ᐋᔾᔨᒌᖕᖏᓐᓂᖏᑦ ᑐᑯᒥᐊᒃᑭᑦ

ᐊᕝᕙᓂᓕᐅᖕᒪᑕ ᐋᔾᔨᒌᖏᓐᓂᖏᑦ ᐋᔾᔨᙳᐊᒃ. ᑕᑯᔪᓐᓇᖅᐱᒋᑦ?

ᑎᑎᕋᕐᓂᕿᓴᐅᑎᑎᑦᑎᓂᖅ!

ᐅᓂᒃᑳᓕᐅᕆᑦ ᓇᐃᑦᑐᕐᒥᒃ (ᒪᒃᐱᒐᖅ ᐊᑕᐅᓯᖅ ᓇᐃᓐᓂᖅᓴᕐᔫᓐᓃᑦ) ᐃᓄᒃᑎᑐᑦ ᖃᓪᓗᓈᑎᑐᓪᔫᓐᓃᑦ ᓇᓄᐃᑦ ᒥᒃᓴᓄᑦ. ᐊᑐᓚᐅᖅᓯᒪᔾᕐᓂᓪᔫᓐᓃᑦ ᐅᓂᒃᑳᙶᐊᕐᒥᓪᔫᓐᓃᑦ. ᐊᑕᐅᓯᖅ ᐅᓂᒃᑳᓕᐊᖑᓯᒪᔪᖅ ᓴᖅᑭᑕᐅᒐᔾᖅᑐᖅ ᑎᑎᖅᑐᒐᖅᓯᒪᓗᓂ ᐅᖃᓕᒫᒐᐅᓛᖅᑐᒥᒃ. ᐆᑦᑐᑦᑕᓕᓂᑦᓕ!

ᐅᓂᒃᑳᑦ ᓇᒃᓯᐅᑎᔪᓐᓇᖅᑕᐃᑦ ᖃᕋᓴᐅᔭᒃᑯᑦ ᐅᕗᖓ: youth@qia.ca ᓇᓗᓇᐃᕐᓗᒍ ‘ᑳᑯᓗᒃ ᑎᑎᕋᕐᓂᕿᓴᐅᑎᓂᖅ’ ᖁᓛᒍᑦ.

ᓇᒃᓯᐅᑎᓗᒎᓐᓃᑦ ᑎᑎᖅᑲᑎᒍᑦ ᐅᕗᖓ:
‘ᑳᑯᓗᒃ ᑎᑎᕋᕐᓂᕿᓴᐅᑎᓂᖅ’
ᕿᑭᖅᑕᓂ ᐃᓄᐃᑦ Association P.O. Box 1340 Iqaluit, NU X0A 0H0

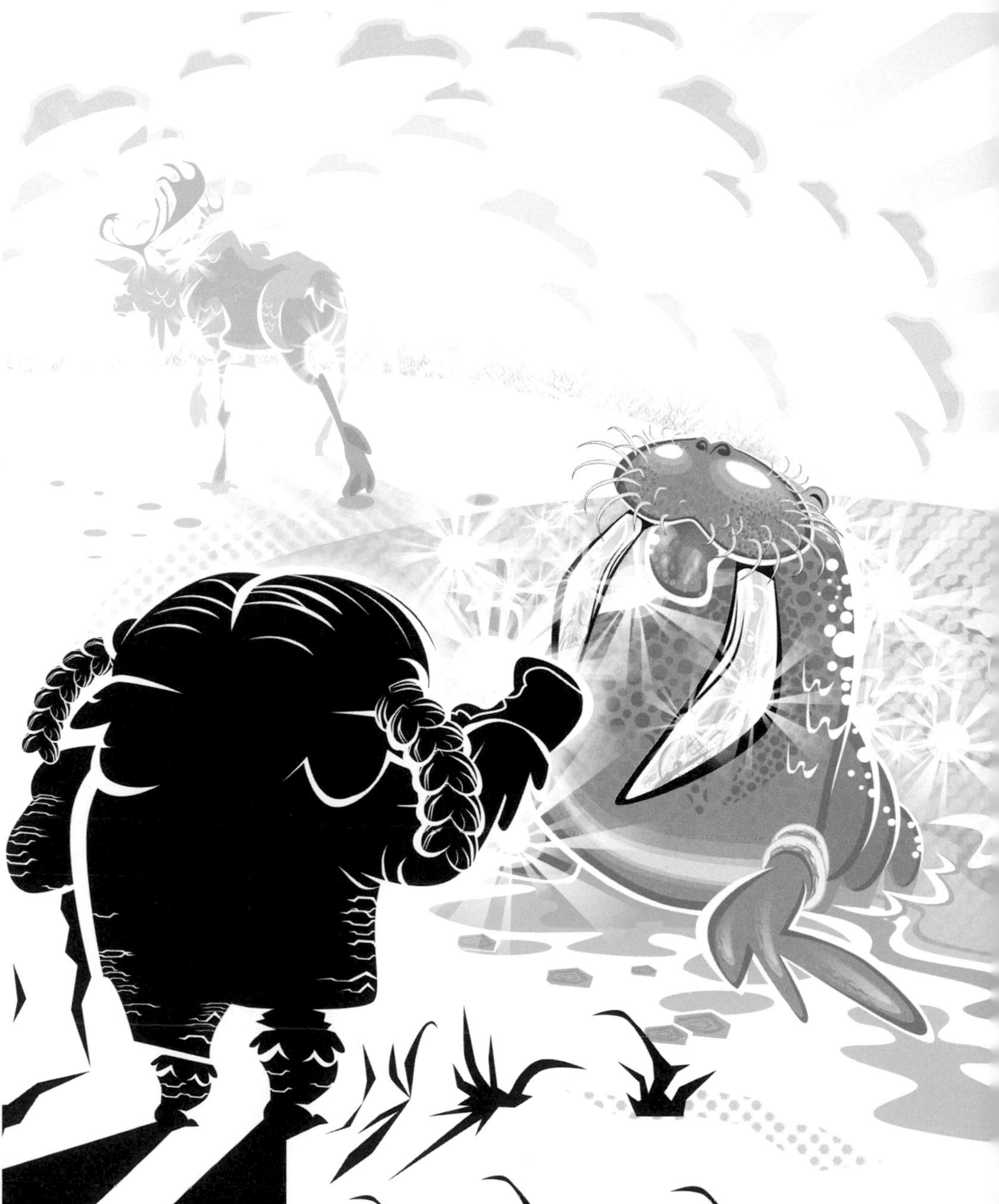

ᑕᕝᕙᓂ ᑕᐃᒫᒃ ᐊᐃᕖᑦ ᑐᒃᑐᐃᓪᓗ ᓄᓇᑦᑎᓐᓃᓕᕐᓂᖅᐸᑦ.

ᐅᓪᓗᐃᑦ ᐃᓚᖕᒐᓐᓂᒃ ᑐᒃᑐ ᑕᑯᓪᓗᓂ ᐊᖑᓇᓱᑎᒥᒃ ᐊᒡᒋᖅᑐᒥᒃ. ᑐᒃᑑᑉ ᑲᑉᐱᐊᒋᓇᓂᐅᒃ ᐊᖑᑦ, ᐸᖕᒐᓚᖕᕕᒋᒐᒥᐅᒃ ᐋᓐᓂᖅᑐᓂᐅᒃ ᑑᒑᕐᒥᓄᑦ ᐊᖑᓇᓱᒃᑎ. ᐊᖑᓇᓱᒃᑎ ᐅᓪᓚᐃᓐᓇᖅᑐᓂ ᓄᓇᒥᓄᑦ ᐅᖅᑲᐅᑎᕙᐃᑦ ᖃᓄᐃᕋᑖᕐᓂᕐᒥᓂᒃ.

ᐊᖑᓇᓱᒃᑎ ᐅᓂᒃᑲᐅᔾᔨᒐᒥ ᓂᖕᒋᐅᕿᓗᖕᒥᒃ ᑲᑉᐱᐊᓱᐊᓂᕆᕋᑖᖅᑕᒥᓂᒃ, ᓂᖖᒐᒃᑐᐊᓘᓪᓗᓂ ᓂᖕᒋᐅᖅ.

ᐃᓯᒫᓄᓗ ᐅᖅᑲᓕᓪᓗᓂ, "ᖃᕐᓘᖃᖅᑕ ᑐᒃᑐᖅᖄᑕᐅᖅᐳᖃᖃᑉ!"
ᑕᐱᒪᐊᑐᒃᑎᖅᑎᑐᓂᐅᒃᓗ: ᑐᒃᑐᓚᐅᖅᖄᐳᖅᖄ. ᐊᓴᒪᐅᓂ, ᑕᑯᓕᒥᐅᖅ
ᐄᓴᓕᑎᐊᖅᑐᒐᓇᐅᖅ. ᑕᖀᑯᓂ, ᖃᖓᓂᐆᖅᔾᓄ ᐆᓀᓄᖅ
ᖅᐱᐳᓴᑎᖅᐄ. ᐄᓴᓕᑎᐊᖅᐆᔾᓕᓲᖅᑐᓂᓗ.

ᒡᓗᕿᑦᖄᕈᔭᕿᓴᐅᓛᖅᓕᖕ ᐳᓇᑕᓇᒡᑎᕚ ᐊᐃᒪᒡᔪᕐᐊ
ᖏᒡᑎᕿᓴᐅᑐᒡᖅᕕ ᒡᕙᑦ ᓂᓇᐸᖅᓴᐊ ᓄᕐᑕᖅ ᓇᔾᖑᒡ
ᑕᐅᖅᓴᖅᖏᒡᑐᒧᕙ ᒡᕙᑦ ᓃᓇᑉᒥᑕᖅᓴᑕᕋᓄᒧᐊ, ᑕᑕᒡᑲᖅ
ᒡᕙᑦ, "ᖅᐃᖅᕿᓴᔪ ᐊᐅᖅᓴᕈᑕᖅᑕᔪᓂ"

ᖃᓄᖅ ᑐᒃᑐ ᐊᐃᕙᕐᓚ ᐱᙳᕐᓂᒪᖕᖏᑎᒃ

ᐋᓐᑕᓂ ᐱᑕᐊᓐ

ᐅᓂᒃᑳᖅ ᐅᓇ ᐊᑐᓚᐅᖅᑐᕙᓂᖅ ᐊᕐᕌᒍᒐᓵᓗᐃᑦ ᐊᓂᒍᖅᓯᒪᓕᖅᑐᑦ ᐅᑭᐅᖅᑕᖅᑐᒥ.

ᑕᐃᒃᓯᒪᓂ, ᓂᖏᐅᕈᓗᒃ ᐃᒃᓯᕚᓪᓗᓂ ᐊᖏᕐᕋᒥᓂ ᐃᓱᒪᐅᔭᖅᑐᕙᓂᖅ ᐃᒻᒥᓄᑦ: "ᐆᒪᔪᖅᑖᒃᑲᓐᓂᕆᐊᖅᑲᖅᑐᒍᑦ ᐊᖑᓇᓱᒃᓴᑦᑎᓐᓂ. ᐆᒪᔪᖅᑖᒃᑲᓐᓂᕆᐊᖅᑲᖅᑐᒍᑦ ᓂᕆᔭᐅᓂᐊᖅᑐᓂᒃ ᐃᓚᑦᑎᓐᓄᑦ ᐊᓐᓄᕌᒃᓴᑦᑎᓐᓂᓪᓗ ᐅᖅᑰᔭᕐᑎᒃᓴᑦᑎᓐᓂᒃ ᐅᑭᐅᒃᑯᑦ."

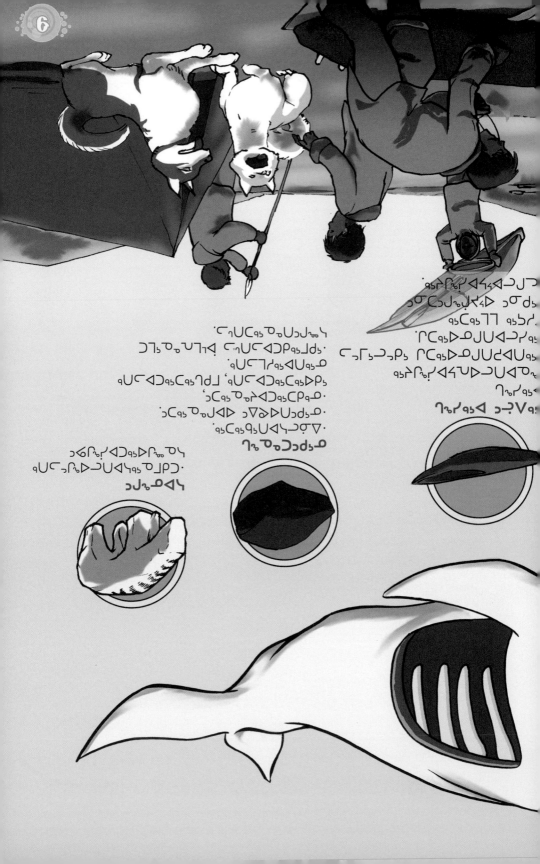

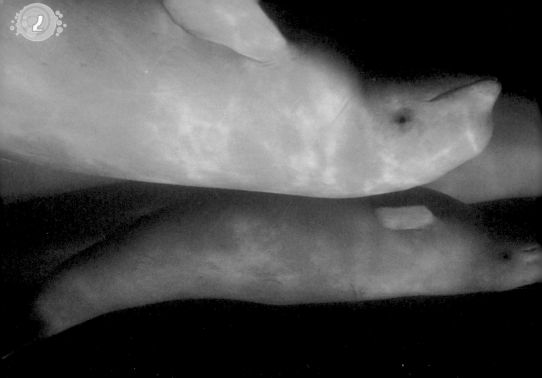

ᐃᕗᒐᖅᓯᒪᔪᖅ ᐱᐊᕋᑉ ᓴᐅᒥᐊ

ᐃᑦᑕᕐᓕᐅᑉᑕᖃᖅᐸᐅᕐᒥᐅᒍᒐᔅᒍ ᑭᓇᓪᓕᕐᕕ ᓯᖅᓯᖅᖅᐅᐱᒍᓪᖃᖃᐅ᠎ᕐᒍᑉ᠎
ᐅᑕᖅᐊᖅᐊᐅᑉ ᖃᐅᐱᐊ ᓂᒌᖅᑎᓕᐊᒎ ᓯᖃᑕᖃᖅᖅᐁᕗᑖᐸ ᕏᐸᕏᖅᖅᐸᖑᖅᖅᓯᒪᖅᑕᐃ

ᖃᐅᑉ ᓄᖅᑳᑦ ᖅᑲᓗᒍᐱᐊᑦ
ᐊᔨᖅᑯᑎᓐᑦ ᑭᒃᒍᑎᓐ ᒍᑦ

ᐊ ᓇᖅ ᑕᑯᑦᖃᖅᐸᑦ?

ᖅ◻◻◻ᖅ ᒥᒣᑐᖕᖅ, ᑭᒍᑎᓐᑦ
ᒥᐱᑐ◻ᒃᑯᑦᖅᑕᓐ ᑭᐊᕐᐊᒍᖏᖅ
ᐃᑐᑭᐅᑭᖅᒥᑦ. ᑎᑕᒍᑕᖃᖅᖅᑐᖅ,
ᓂ◻ᓂᖅᐊ◻◻ᒍᖌᕐᒐᒨᑦ.
ᖅᑲ◻◻◻ᖅ ᐊᒪᐅᔭᖏᕐᑦᒐᖅ.
ᓂᒃ◻◻ᖏ ᐅᖃᓵᓐᑐᖅ
ᒨᓗᖅᑉ◻ᑐᒨᓗ ᓂᐊᕐᒃᓄᑐᑦ ᖅᖕᖕᖕᖎ.
ᓴᖅᐊᓯᖏᑎᒍᖏᕐᑦᑐᑦ, ᖅᑲᓄᖅᖕᖅᑕᐸᖅ
ᖅᑐᖕᒥᖅ ᑐᓂᓌᓐᐊᒥᑦᖅ. ᖅᑲᓄᖅᖕᖅᑕᖅ
ᐃᖅ◻◻ᓐᖏ, ᖅᑐᓂᕐᒨᖏ.ᖅᖅᑐᓂ.

ᖅᖅᐅᓄᖅᑕᑦ ᑕᑐᓂᖅᑕᖂᓇᖅᑐᑦ 5
ᒥᑐᓴᑦ ᒥᕐᑑᒃᕐᑦ ᓴᖅᐊᒥᑭᖅᑲᓐᒪᓐᒨᑦ.
ᑎᒎ◻ ᐅᖅᑐᒎᐊ◻ᓂᖅᐊᒨᖅᑐᑦ
136◻◻◻ᓂᒍᒃᖕᓂᑦᖅᖕ. ᐊᖅᑫᖂᑐᑦ
ᖅᐅᖅ◻◻ᖕᖅᑕᑦ ᒥᒣᓂᖅᖕᓯᒌᖇᑦ,
ᐅᖅᑐᒣᖕᖂᖅᑕᒨᖕᖅᑐᑦ 900 ᒨᓗᒑᓐᓂᖅᖕ.

ᐊᓕᒍᑎᖅᖅᐸᑦ?

◻ᖅᐅᖅ◻◻ᖅᑕᑦ ᒨᑭᓯᖅᖅᐅᑦ
341◻◻◻ᓄᖕᓇᑦ ᐃᓄᐊᖑᓂ. ᑕᑕ◻
◻◻◻ᑎᓂᕐᐊᑦ ᐊᖅᑐᑭᕐᒨᖕᑦ
◻◻ᓐᖅᑐᖌᓗ, ᑕᒨᐊᓗᑎᑦ. ᖅᑲᓄᖅᖕᖅᑕᑦ
ᐊᖅᑐᑭᕐᒨᖕᑦ ᐃᓄᐊᑕᑦ◻ᒍᓐᑦ ᐊᔪᔨᒨᖅᑦ.

ᐊ.ᐱᑎᐊᖅᐸᖕᑦᖃᖅᖕᑦ ᐊᔪᖅᒨᓂᖅ?

ᐃ, ᖅᑲ◻◻ᖅᑕᑦ ᑲᓐᒪᒨᖂᓪᑐᖅᖕ.
ᑲᑎᓂᖅ◻◻◻ᑦ ᖂᑐᐅᑐᓐᑦ.
ᖅᑲᐅᖅ◻◻ᑕᑦ ᑲᓐᒪᒨᖏ ᑕᐊᔨᐅᖅᑦ
ᖅᖂᑐᖂᑐᑦ ◻ᒐᑦᖕ. ᑲᓐᒪᒨᖏᖅᖕᑦ
ᑎᑕᐃᐊᓐᖅᑎᐊᑦ ᐅᑕᐊᒦᓗ.
ᖅᑲᐅᖅᖅ◻◻ᑕᑦ ᐊᖅᑐᓗᕐᒥᐊᔪᖅᑦ
ᑲᑎ◻◻◻ᑐᖅᖕ ◻ᖂᑕᖅᑐᑦᖏᓗ. ᐊᓐᓐᑦ,
ᖅᑲ◻◻◻ᑕᑦ ◻ᖂᑕᖅᖂᓐᒥᒦᖅᖕ,
ᑲᑎᕐ◻◻◻ᒐᑐᖌᐊᕐᑦ
ᑲᑎᒦᖅᓇᐅᖂᖅᖂᑐᓐᑦ, 10,000ᓂᖅᖕ
ᐊᒦᕐᒨᖕᖕᐅᖂᖅᑐᑦ.

ᐊ.ᓪᖅᑲᑎᓐᖅᑦ ᐳᐃᖅᖅᖂᑐᓐᖅ?

ᐊᖅᑲ, ᖅᑲᐅᖅᖅᓄᖅᑕᑦ ᓯᖅᑲᐃᑐᕐᑐᖌᖕᑦ
ᓴᖅᑲᐊᑎᖅᖂᑲᑎᒨᓐᖅᑎᕐᑦᕐᑦᑕᕐᑦ.
ᐃᖕᐃᕐᖅᑲᖑᖕᖅ 3ᒦ 9 ᒨ ᐳᒦᒥᕐᖏᓂᖅᖕ
ᐃᑕᖅᖅᖅᖂ. ᑕᒪᓗᐊᒦᐊᖅᖕᖃᖏᓂᒌᒦ,
ᓪᖕᑕᕐᖏᖅᑕᓐ◻ᖏᖅᖕᖅᑐᑦ 22 ᐳᒦᒥᕐᖏᓂᖅᖕ
ᐃᑕᖅᖅᖅᖂ, ᖅᑯᑉᒦᒦᕐᐅᓄᓗᐊᖅᖕ.

ᐊ.ᓄᐱᑭᕐᔭᒍᐊᑦ?

ᐃ! ᖅᑲᐅᖅᖅᓄᖅᑕᑦ ᓄᐱᑯᕐᐅᖅᖂᕐᔪᐅᑦ
ᐊᒦᖅᑕᕐᑦᒨᓂᖅᖕ. ᔭᐅᔨᐱᒨᖕᖅᑐᖌᖂᓂᖅᖕ
ᓄᐱᑭᕐᔭᒍᕐᑦ, ᑯᒃᖅᑯᐊᖂᓪᕐᑦᑎᓐ◻ᓐᖅᖕ,
ᐃᖅᖂᐅᓐᓐ◻ᓐᖅᖕ, ᐳᐊᖕᒦᐊᖂᖅᖅᐅᑕᓂᖅᖅᖂᖕ.
ᔪᑭᔭᐊᖏᖅᑎᓐᓐᔭᓄᑦ◻
ᐃᒦᓂᐅᖅᑦᒨᖂᓗᐊᖅᖕ. ᖅᑲᐅᖅᖅᓄᖅᑕᑦ
ᓄᐱᑭᖕᐊᓐᖅᓴᖅᖕᓄᖕ ᐊᑦ,
ᑕᐃᖂᐅᔨᖂᔪᒨᖂᖂᑕᕐᔭᑦ, "ᐃᓄᐊᑉ
ᖂᑐᔪᐊᖅᖕᑦ." ᖅᑲᐅᖅᖅᓄᖅᑕᑦ
ᓄᐊᒦᖕᐊᖕᑦ ᐊᑐᖂᖕᑐᓐᖅ ᐊᔪᒌᖂᕐᒨᓂᖕ
ᐊᓄᑦᔨᕐᔭᐅᖅᑦ, ᐊᓂᖂᖅᓯᐊᖅᕐᒨᖕᖕᓂᖅᖕ ᔭᑯᑕᑦ
ᐊᓄᐊᓂᒥᒐᓐᓗ ᖅᑲᐅᖂᔭᖂᐱᕐᓐᖂᕐᔭᑦ
ᐃᓐᖂᕐᒦ, ᑕᖅᑐᒦᒦ ᐊᓪᓂ. ᖅᑲᐅᖅᖅᓄᖅᑕᑦ
ᖂᑉᑕᖅᑕᖅᖅᖂᖂᑐᓐᖅ ᐂᒨᔪᖅᖕ◻
ᔪᖂᕐᑦᓐᑎ◻ᑦᓐᑎᑦ ᐊᖂᖂᖕᖅᓂᓂᖅᖕ.
ᔭᑦᓐᔭ◻ᓂ◻ᓂ◻ᖕᖅ ᖅᑲᐅᖂᔭᖂᓐᖅ
ᔪᖂᖂᓐᑕᔨᔪᖂᖅᓐᖂᑦ ᖂᑉᑕᖅᑕᖅᖂ◻ᔪᐊᑦ
ᐅᑎᓐᔨᔪᖂᖕᖅᓗᖕᑦ. ᑕᓂᐊ ᑕᐃᖂᐅᔨᖂᖕ
ᐊᖅᐹᖏᖂᖕᑦ ᓇᓐᖂᖂᖕᖅᓗᖕᑦ ᖅᑲᐅᖅᖂᖕ.

ᐊ.ᐊᖅᑲᖂᐃᑉᖂᑉᐅᖂᑦ?

ᐃ, ᖅᑲᐅᖅᖅᓄᖅᑕᑦ ᐊᖅᑲᖂᐃᑕᒦᖂᓇᖅᑐᖌᑦ
650 ᒥᒦᖂᖅᖕ ᐃᓄᓂᖂᖂᖕᓂᖅᖕ, ᑭᖂᑕᖂ
ᐊᖅᑲᖂᐃᓪᖂᖂᖂᖅᖂᑎᑦ 20 ᒥᒦᖂᖕᖕ
ᐃᓄᓂᖂᖂᖂᑐᑦ ᓂᖂᖂᐃᑕᖂᖂᔨᖂᖅᖂᖅᑐᖕᑦ.
ᐊᖅᑲᖂᐃᑕᒦᖂᖂᖕᖅ 20 ᒦᖂᓂᖂᖕᑦ.
ᐊᖅᑲᖂᐃᑕᒦᖂᖂᓂᒐᖕᑦ, ᖅᑲᐅᖅᖅᓄᖅᑕᑦ
ᖂᑐᖂᖂᖕᖅ◻ᖅᖂᖕᖅ 2.5 ᐳᒦᒥᕐᖏᖕᖕᑦ
ᐊᓂᖅᖂᖂᖂᐊᑕᑐᖂᐅᖂᖂᖅᑕᖂᓯᖕᖅ.

ᐊ.ᖅᑲᖂᓐᖏ ᐊᑐᓂᐅᖂᑎᔨᖅᖕ ᐅᒦᖂᔪᒍᑦ?
ᖅᑲᐅᖅᖅᓄᖅᑕᑦ ᐅᒦᒦᖂᖕᑐᑦ 25ᓂᖕ
ᐊᖂᖂᑐᓂᖕᖕ 30ᓂᖕᑦ.

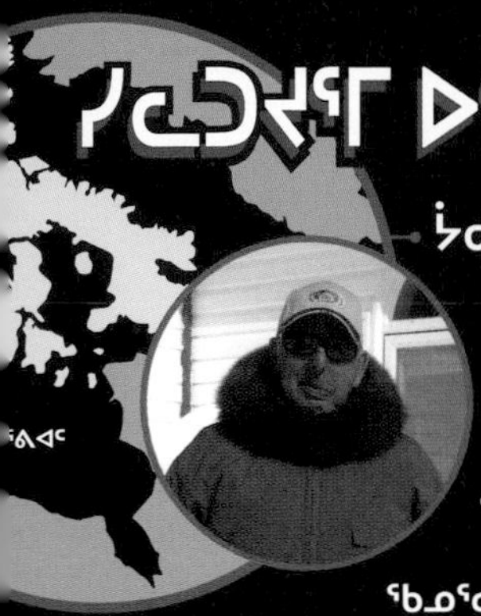

ᓯᓚᑐᔪᕐᒥ ᐅᕐᑲᐅᔾᔫᓯᐊᑦ

ᓵᓂ ᖃᕆᑕᕐᒥ

ᓵᓂ ᖃᕆᑕᖅ ᐃᓐᓇᐅᔪᖅ ᐊᕐᕕᐊᕐᒥᐅᑕᖅ. ᐊᐃᑐᕆᐊᓇ ᐱᐅᔪᖅ ᑯᓯᒐᐅᑉ ᐊᐱᖅᓱᖅᑕᕕᓂᖓ ᖃᐅᔨᓴᖅᑕᐃᑦ ᒥᒃᓵᓄᑦ. ᐊᐱᖅᓱᕐᓂᑯᖕᒋᑕ ᐃᓚᖓᓃᙱᖅᑐᖅ ᑕᕝᕙ.

ᖃᓄᑎᒋ ᕿᓚᓗᒐᕆᓯᖃᑦᑕᖅᓯᒪᓚᖅᐱᑦ?
ᐊᕐᕼᒍᖃᖅᑎᓪᓗᖓ ᑕᓪᓚᒪᓂᒃ ᐊᕐᕕᓂᓚᖕᓂᓪᓘᓐᓃᑦ ᐃᓚᐅᖃᑦᑕᓚᐅᖅᓯᒪᔪᖓ ᕿᓚᓗᒐᕆᓯᕆᐊᖅᑐᓄᑦ. ᑕᑯᓐᓇᖅᑐᖓ, ᓇᐅᑦᑎᖅᓱᖅᑐᖅᑐᖓ, ᐃᑲᔪᖅᑐᖓᓗ ᕿᓚᓗᒐᕆᓲᑐᓂᒃ.

ᖃᓄᕐᓕ ᐊᔾᔨᒌᙱᑎᒋᓕᖅᐸᒃ ᑕᐃᒃᓯᒪᓂ ᒫᓐᓇᒧᑦ?
ᐊᓯᔾᔨᒍᐊᖅᓯᒪᖏᑦᑑᒐᓗᐊᖅ ᑭᓯᐊᓂ ᒫᓇ ᐅᔾᔨᖅᓱᑎᐊᖏᓐᓂᖅᓴᐅᔮᓕᖅᑐᑦ ᕿᓚᓗᒐᕆᐊᖅᑐᑦ. ᐳᖅᓱᐃᖅᓯᒍᐊᖃᑦᑕᖅᑕᓕᖅᑐᑦ ᐃᓄᐃᑦ. ᐅᖅᓱᖅ ᒪᒃᑖᕐᒥᒃ ᒪᒪᕐᓂᖅᓴᐅᑎᑦᑎᕙᖕᒪᑦ. ᐅᖅᓱᖃᖏᒧᐊᖅᑎᓪᓗᒍ ᒪᖕᒋᖕᓂᖅᓴᐅᕙᖕᒪᑦ ᓱᑭᖅᓴᕋᐃᓐᓂᖅᓴᐅᓪᓗᓂᓗ. ᐅᖅᓲᑉ ᒪᒪᕐᓂᖅᓴᐅᑎᒃᐸᖕᒪᒍ. ᐊᖑᓇᓱᒃᑏᑦ ᒫᓇᐅᔪᖅ ᐳᖃᓱᖑᓕᕐᒪᑕ ᐅᕐᑯᒪᐃᑎᑦᑎᓗᐊᓲᖑᒻᒪᑕᒎᖅ, ᑭᓯᐊᓂ ᑎᐱᑦᑎᐊᕆᑎᑦᑎᖅᑕᑦᑕᖅᑐᑦ ᒪᒃᑖᕐᒥᒃ.

ᐳᖅᑲᓕᑦᑕᕐᒥᖕᒪᑕ ᖃᐅᔾᔭᖅᑕᐃᖅᒎᖅ ᐃᙳᒋᓲᑦ. ᑐᓴᓚᐅᖅᓯᒪᕕᒋᑦ ᖃᓄᕐᓗ ᓂᐱᖃᓲᖑᕙᑦ?
ᐃ, ᑐᓴᓚᐅᖅᓯᒪᔭᒃᑲ. ᐊᖑᓇᓱᒃᑎᓂᒃ ᖃᐅᔾᔭᖅᑕᐃᑦ ᖃᐅᔾᔨᙱᑐᐊᕌᖓᑕ ᑐᓴᖅᓴᐅᓱᑦ ᐃᒃᑲᖕᓂᕐᒦᒃᑐᑎᒃ. ᑐᓴᕐᑎᒍ ᐳᐸᒃᑕᐅᑎᒋᖃᑦᑕᙱᑕᕗᑦ. ᐅᓕᓕᕐᐃᒻᒪᑦ ᑭᓯᐊᓂ. ᐳᐃᔮᕋᖓᑕ ᐃᓛᓐᓂᑦ ᐅᕕᙱᐊᓱᑦ. ᓱᕐᓗᖕᒐᑎᒍᑦ ᓴᙳᐊᖅᑑᔭᓲᑦ.

ᑲᐅᔾᔭᖅᑕᐃᑦ ᐊᖑᓇᓱᒐᕐᓂᙱᓕᑦ?
ᐃᖑ ᓇᕐᒥᔪᖅ ᑭᓯᐊᓂ ᐃᒃᑲᖕᓂᕐᒧᑦ ᐅᖑᐊᕆᐊᖅᖃᑕᑦ. ᓇᒧᙱᓚᕐᓯᐊᕐᒪᖕᖠᑕ ᖃᐅᔭᓭᔪᒋᑦ ᕿᓄᐃᔩᕈᓐᓇᕆᐊᓕᒃ. ᐳᖑᐊᕆᐊᓖᑦ ᐃᒃᑲᖕᓂᕐᒧᑦ. ᐅᖔᕐᔪᒋᑦ ᒪᓕᒡᔪᒋᑦ ᐃᒃᑲᕐᓇᑦᑕᐃᓕᒪᒋᐊᖃᓪᓗᓂ ᐃᒃᑲᖕᓂᒃᑯᕐᔪᓂ.

ᑲᓄᐃᓕᐅᕆᐊᖅᑳᖅ ᐊᓐᓇᐃᑦᑕᐃᓕᒪᓇᓯᐊᕐᔪᓂ ᐊᖑᓇᓯᐊᕐᔪᒥ?
ᐃᒃᑲᓐᓂᕐᔫᖅᑎᓐᓇᓯᒋᐊᓖᑦ. ᒫᓂᓕ ᑭᕙᓪᓕᕐᒥ ᐃᒃᑲᖕᒪᑦ ᓂᐱᑭᑦᑑᓇᓯᒋᐊᓕᒃ. ᕿᓚᓗᒐᐃᑦ ᑐᓴᑦᑎᐊᖅᑐᐊᓘᔭᕐᒪᑕ ᐅᒥᐊᕐᓂᒃ ᐊᖑᓇᓱᒃᑎᓂᓪᓗ ᖃᓂᑦᑐᖅᑲᓕᕖᙶᕐᒪᑦ ᑐᓵᔫᑦ ᓂᐱᒃᑭᐅᓗᐊᓕᕐᐃᒪᒪᑕ. ᖃᐅᔨᒪᔫᖑᒐᒪᑦ ᐆᒪᔪᕐᓂᐊᓕᕚᖕᒪᑦ. ᕿᓚᓗᒐᕆᓯᐊᖅᑕᐃᑦ ᖃᐅᔨᒪᓇᓯᕆᐊᖃᖅᑕᐃᑦ ᑕᐃᓐᓇᑐᐊᕐᓗ ᐱᓇᓯᐊᕐᓗᒍ. ᒪᒃᑯᕐᓂᖅᓴᐃᑦ ᒪᒪᕐᓂᖅᐹᑦ. ᑲᐅ... ᖅᑐᐃᓐᓇᐅᖕᒋᑦᑐᑦ ᐃᓱᖅᑕᐃᓐᓇᐅᒻᒥᒐᑎᒃᓗ.

ᑭᓚᐃᑦ ᒫᓇ ᖃᔾᔫᓇᐅᓂᖅᓴᐅᓯᓇᓕᖅᐱᒋᑦ ᑕᐃᒃᓯᒪᓂᓂᑦ ᐅᕙᔪᓐᓃᑦ ᐊᔾᔨᑐᐃᓐᓇᐸᓗᒋᕙᐃᑦ?
ᑕᐃ... ᒪᓂᓂᓪᓕ ᐊᒥᓲᓂᖅᓴᐅᔮᒻᒪᓇᓕᖅᑐᑦ, ᕿᓚᓗᒐᓱᐊᖅᑕᑦᑕᕆᓐᓂᖅᓴᐅᓕᖅᑐᖓᓕ ᑭᓯᐊᓂ ᐊᒥᓱᐊᔫᔭᓕᖅᑐᑦ. ... ᖅ ᕿᓚᓗᒐᓕᐊᔫᖓᓚᕐ. ᕿᓚᓗᒐᖃᐃᓐᓇᕐᔫᖅᑕᖅᔪᖕᒥᔪᖅ, ᑭᓯᐊᓂᑦᑕᐅᖅ ᑕᐅᕗᖕᒐᐃᓐᓇᖕᒋᓐᓂᖅᓴᐅᓕᕐᔪᑦ. ...ᖑᓇᓱᒃᑏᖅᑲᐃ ᑕᐅᕗᖕᒐᐅᔭᐃᓐᓇᓕᕐᓂᖕᒋᓐᓄᑦ, ᐊᓯᐊᓅᖕᖡᖃᑦᑕᓕᖅᑐᑦ.

...ᑯᓪᓗ ᕿᓚᓗᒐᐃᑦ ᐅᖅᓱᖃᕐᓂᖅᓴᐅᕙᒃᐸᑦ?
ᐳᑭᐅᒃᑯᑦ ᕿᓚᓗᒐᐃᑦ ᐅᖅᓱᖃᕐᓂᖅᓴᐅᓲᑦ.' ᖃᐅᔨᓇᓲᖅ ᖁᐃᓐᓂᐅᒐᐃᒻᒪᑕ ᑭᕙᖃᑦᑕᕆᒻᒪᑕ.

...ᑯᓪᓗ ᕿᓚᓗᒐᕋᓱᒋᐊᖓ ᐱᐅᓂᖅᐸᐅᕙ?
...ᓯᐳᐊᑉ ᕿᑎᖅᐸᓯᐊᓂ ᓄᖑᐊᓂᓪᓗᓐᓂᑦ ᐱᒋᐊᕐᓂᖓᓄᑦ ᓯᑎᐱᕆᐅᑉ ᕿᓚᓗᒐᐃᑦ ᒪᒪᕐᓂᖅᐸᐅᓕᖅᑎᓪᓗᒋᑦ.

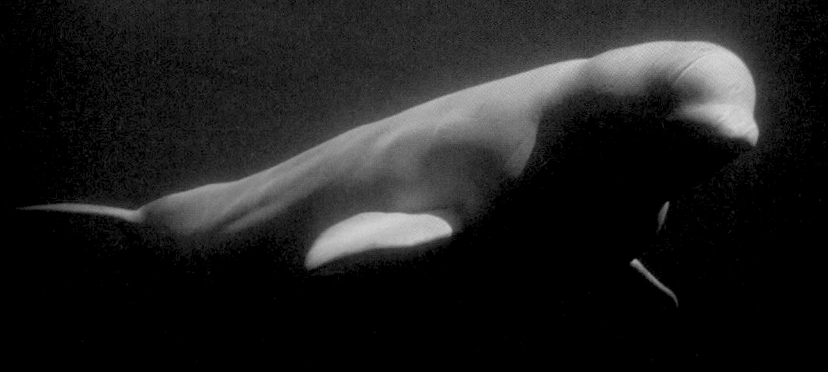

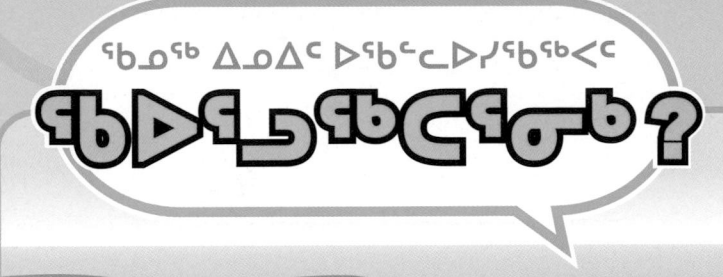

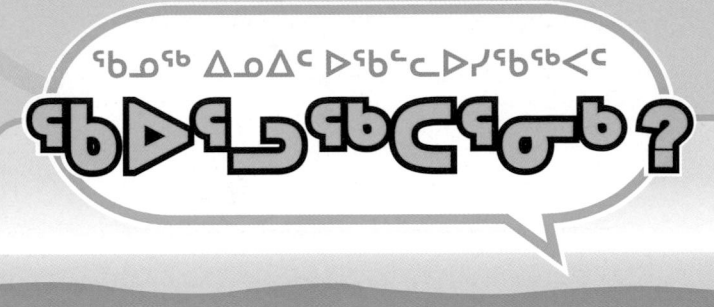

ᕿᑲᓇᖅ ᐃᓄᐃᑦ ᐅᖃᓪᓚᐅᓯᖃᖅᐸᑦ

ᖃᐅᕐᔪᖅᑕᕐᓂᒃ?

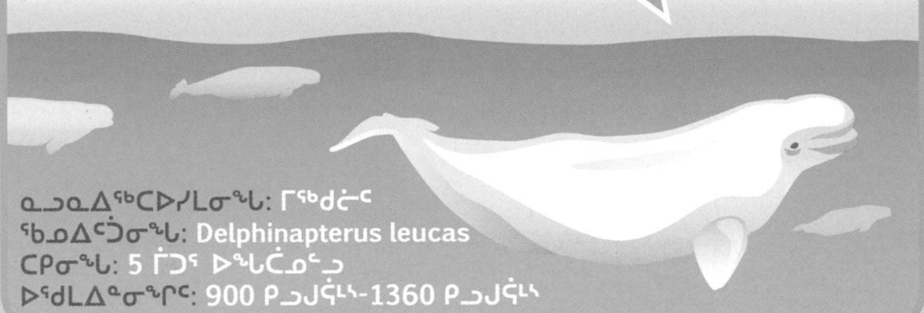

ᓇᓗᓇᐃᖅᑕᐅᓯᒪᓂᖓ: ᒥᖅᑯᓖᑦ
ᖃᓄᐃᑦᑑᓂᖓ: Delphinapterus leucas
ᑕᑭᓂᖓ: 5 ᒦᑐᕐ ᐅᖓᑖᓄᑦᑐ
ᐅᕐᑯᒪᐃᓐᓂᖏᑦ: 900 ᑭᓗᒍᕆᒻᔅ-1360 ᑭᓗᒍᕆᒻᔅ

“ᑕᑯᓚᐅᖅᓯᒪᔪᖓ ᓴᖅᐱᓕᖕᓂᒃ ᑕᓚᕘᓴᒃᑯᑦ ᐊᒻᒪ ᑭᙵᖕᓂ. ᓴᖅᐱᓖᑦ ᐱᐅᒋᔭᒃᑲ.” ᓇᐃᐅᒥ ᑯᕐᓕ, ᐃᖃᓗᐃᑦ

“ᓂᕆᓚᐅᖅᓯᒪᔪᖓ ᓴᖅᐱᓕᕚᓂᖏᒃ, ᖁᐊᖏᒃ. ᐊᐅᓪᓚᖅᓯᒪᑎᓪᓗᑕ ᐊᐅᓱᐃᕙᑐᕐᒧᑦ, ᓴᖅᐱᓕᖓᓖᓗᖕᓂᒃ ᑕᑯᓚᐅᖅᓯᒪᔪᖓ. ᖁᖅᓱᐸᓗᒃᑐᓂᒃ-ᖁᖅᓱᐊᖓᔪᓂᒡᓗ ᑯᒪᖃᓚᐅᖅᓯᒪᔪᑦ (ᓴᖅᐱᓖᑦ).” ᓇᑖᓴ ᒫᑦᓕᓐ, ᐊᕿᐊᕈᖅ

“ᓴᖅᐱᓖᑦ ᐃᖃᓗᒃᑐᓱᑦ. ᐃᓄᐃᑦ ᓴᖅᐱᓕᖓᓱᐊᓱᑦ ᓂᕆᓂᐊᖅᑕᒥᓂᒃ. ᓂᕆᓚᐅᖅᓯᒪᔪᖓ.”
ᓵᓴ ᐃᐊᔾᓈᓴ, ᐃᖃᓗᐃᑦ

“ᐃᓄᓕᒫᑲᓴᐃᑦ ᓴᖅᐱᓕᒃᑐᓱᑦ ᓱᖃᐃᒻᒪ ᒪᒪᖅᑐᐊᓗᐃᑦ!” ᑐᓅᓴ ᕿᐊᑦᓯᒃ, ᐃᖃᓗᐃᑦ

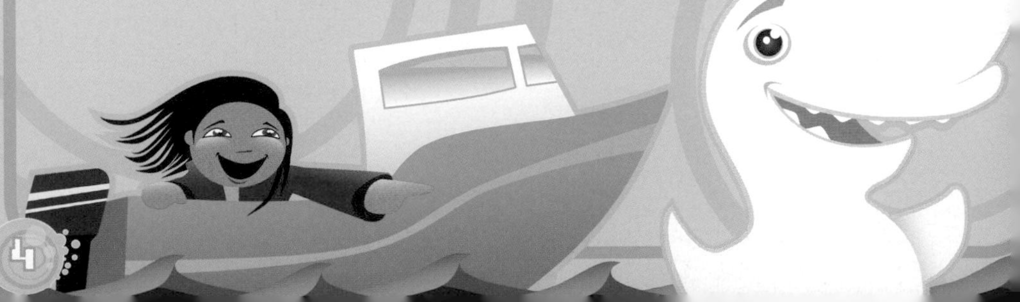

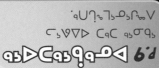

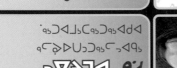
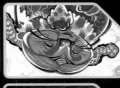

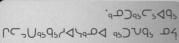